PRAYERS AGAINST THE POWERS OF DARKNESS

Concordat cum originali:
✠ Wilton D. Gregory
Chairman, USCCB Committee on Divine
Worship after review by Rev. Andrew Menke
Executive Director, USCCB Secretariat of
Divine Worship

Published by authority of the Committee on
Divine Worship, United States Conference of
Catholic Bishops

This book contains Appendix II of *Exorcisms and
Related Supplications.*

ISBN 978-1-60137-567-4

First printing, September 2017
Second printing, November 2017

SUPPLICATIONS WHICH MAY BE USED BY THE FAITHFUL PRIVATELY IN THEIR STRUGGLE AGAINST THE POWERS OF DARKNESS

Prayers

HAVE MERCY, LORD GOD,
  on me your servant,
who have become
  like a vessel that is lost
because of the host
  that besieges me.
Deliver me from the
  hands of my enemies
and draw near to me,
that you may seek
  what is lost,
restore to yourself
  what is found,
and not abandon
  what is restored;
so that in all things
  I may be pleasing to you,

by whom I know I have been
  powerfully redeemed.
Through Christ our Lord.
  Amen.

ALMIGHTY GOD,
who give the desolate
  a home to dwell in
and lead prisoners
  into prosperity,
look upon my affliction
and arise in my defense.
Strike down that
  most wicked foe,
so that, after the enemy is
  driven away,
freedom may bring me peace.
And so, restored to tranquil
  devotion,
may I confess how wondrous
  you are,
who have given strength to
  your people.
Though Christ our Lord.
  Amen.

—◦◦◦◦◦◦—

O God,
  creator and defender
  of the human race,
who formed us in
  your own image
and more wonderfully
  recreated us
by the grace of Baptism,
look with favor upon me,
  your servant,
and graciously hear
  my prayers.
May the splendor of
  your glory
dawn in my heart, I pray,
so that with all terror, fear
  and dread removed,
and serene in mind
  and spirit,

I may be able to praise you
with my brothers and sisters
  in your Church.
Through Christ our Lord.
  Amen.

O GOD, AUTHOR OF EVERY
  mercy and all goodness,
who willed your Son to
  submit for our sake
to the yoke of the Cross,
so that you might drive from
  us the power of the enemy,
look with mercy upon my
  lowliness and pain,
and grant, I pray,
that, defeating the onslaught
  of the Evil One,
you will fill with the grace of
  your blessing
the one you made new in the
  font of Baptism.
Through Christ our Lord.
  Amen.

O GOD,
who through the grace
  of adoption
chose me to be a
  child of light,
grant, I pray,
that I may not be shrouded
  in the darkness of
  demons,
but always be seen to stand
in the bright light of
  the freedom
that I have received
  from you.
Through Christ our Lord.
  Amen.

Invocations to the
Most Holy Trinity

GLORY BE to the Father,
and to the Son,
and to the Holy Spirit.

To God alone
 be honor and glory.

LET US BLESS the
  Father and the Son
  with the Holy Spirit;
let us praise and exalt him
  for ever.

WE INVOKE YOU,
  we praise you,
  we adore you,
O blessed Trinity.
Our hope,
  our salvation,
  our glory,
O blessed Trinity.
Deliver me,
  save me,
  give me life,
O blessed Trinity.

HOLY, HOLY, HOLY
  is the Lord God almighty,
who was, and who is,
  and who is to come.
To you be honor and
  dominion, O blessed Trinity,
to you be glory and power
  through ages unending.

To YOU BE PRAISE,
   to you be glory,
to you be thanksgiving
   from age to age,
O blessed Trinity.

HOLY IS GOD!
  Holy and Mighty!
Holy and Immortal One,
  have mercy on me!

Invocations to Our Lord Jesus Christ

A.

Jesus, Son of the living
  God,
> have mercy on me.

Jesus, image of the Father,
> have mercy on me.

Jesus, eternal Wisdom,
> have mercy on me.

Jesus, splendor of the
  eternal light,
> have mercy on me.

Jesus, Word of life,
> have mercy on me.

Jesus, Son of the Virgin Mary,
> have mercy on me.

Jesus, God and man,
　　　have mercy on me.

Jesus, High Priest,
　　　have mercy on me.

Jesus, herald of the
　Kingdom of God,
　　　have mercy on me.

Jesus, the way, the truth
　and the life,
　　　have mercy on me.

Jesus, Bread of Life,
　　　have mercy on me.

Jesus, true vine,
　　　have mercy on me.

Jesus, brother of the poor,
　　　have mercy on me.

Jesus, friend of sinners,
          have mercy on me.

Jesus, physician of soul
  and body,
          have mercy on me.

Jesus, salvation of the
  oppressed,
          have mercy on me.

Jesus, solace of the forsaken,
          have mercy on me.

You came into this world,
          have mercy on me.

You freed those oppressed
  by the devil,
          have mercy on me.

You hung upon the Cross,
	have mercy on me.

You accepted death
  for our sake,
	have mercy on me.

You were laid in the tomb,
	have mercy on me.

You descended into hell,
	have mercy on me.

You rose again from the
  dead,
	have mercy on me.

You ascended into heaven,
	have mercy on me.

You sent the Holy Spirit
  upon the Apostles,
        have mercy on me.

You are seated at the
  right hand of the Father,
        have mercy on me.

You will come to judge the
  living and the dead,
        have mercy on me.

B.

By your Incarnation,
    deliver me, O Lord.

By your Nativity,
    deliver me, O Lord.

By your Baptism and
  holy fasting,
    deliver me, O Lord.

By your Cross and Passion,
    deliver me, O Lord.

By your Death and burial,
    deliver me, O Lord.

By your holy Resurrection,
    deliver me, O Lord.

By your wondrous
  Ascension,
        deliver me, O Lord.

By the outpouring of the
  Holy Spirit,
        deliver me, O Lord.

By your coming in glory,
        deliver me, O Lord.

Other Invocations
to the Lord

When naming the Cross, the faithful may appropriately sign themselves with the Sign of the Cross.

SAVE ME, O CHRIST
   the Savior,
through the power
   of the ✠ Cross.
In the sea you saved Peter,
have mercy on me.

THROUGH THE SIGN
   of the ✠ Cross,
free us from our enemies,
   O Lord our God.

SAVE US
   through your ✠ Cross,
   O Christ the Redeemer,
who by dying destroyed
   our death,
and by rising restored
   our life.

WE ADORE YOUR ✠ CROSS,
    O Lord,
we recall your glorious
    Passion;
you suffered for our sake:
have mercy on us.

WE ADORE YOU, O CHRIST,
  and we bless you,
because by
  your ✠ Holy Cross
you have redeemed
  the world.

Invocations to the Blessed Virgin Mary

WE FLY TO YOUR PROTECTION,
  O holy Mother of God;
despise not our petitions
  in our necessities,
but ever deliver us
  from all danger,
O glorious and
  blessed Virgin.

COMFORTER OF THE AFFLICTED,
  pray for us.
Help of Christians,
  pray for us.

GRANT THAT I MAY PRAISE
   you, holy Virgin;
give me power
   against your enemies.

My Mother, in whom I trust!

O Virgin Mary
  Mother of God,
plead with Jesus for me.

Most noble Queen
  of the world,
Mary ever Virgin,
who bore Christ the Lord
  and Savior of all,
intercede for our peace
  and salvation.

Mary, Mother of grace,
Mother of mercy,
protect us from the enemy,
and receive us at
    the hour of our death.

MOST LOVING VIRGIN MARY,
hasten to my aid
  in all trials,
in my troubles
  and in my needs,
and beg for me
  from your beloved Son
deliverance from every evil
and from all danger
  to soul and body.

REMEMBER, O most gracious
    Virgin Mary,
that never was it known
that anyone who fled
    to your protection,
implored your help, or
    sought your intercession
was left unaided.
Inspired with this confidence,
I fly to you, O Virgin of
    virgins, my Mother.
To you I come,
before you I stand,
    sinful and sorrowful.
O Mother of the
    Word Incarnate,
despise not my petitions,
but in your mercy,
    hear and answer me.

Invocation to Saint Michael the Archangel

SAINT MICHAEL
   THE ARCHANGEL,
   defend us in battle;
be our safeguard against
   the wickedness and snares
   of the devil.
May God rebuke him,
   we humbly pray:
and you, O Prince of the
   heavenly hosts,
by the power of God,
cast down to hell Satan
   and the other evil spirits,
who prowl through the
   world for the ruin of souls.
   Amen.

Litany Prayers

KYRIE, ELEISON.

> Kyrie, eleison.

Christe, eleison.

> Christe, eleison.

Kyrie, eleison.

> Kyrie, eleison.

Or:

LORD, HAVE MERCY.

> Lord, have mercy.

Christ, have mercy.

> Christ, have mercy.

Lord, have mercy.

> Lord, have mercy.

HOLY MARY, Mother of God,

> pray for us (me).

Saint Michael,

> pray for us (me).

Saint Gabriel,
> pray for us (me).

Saint Raphael,
> pray for us (me).

Holy Guardian Angels,
> pray for us (me).

Saint John the Baptist,
> pray for us (me).

Saint Joseph,
> pray for us (me).

Saint Peter,
> pray for us (me).

Saint Paul,
> pray for us (me).

Saint John,
> pray for us (me).

All holy Apostles,
> pray for us (me).

Saint Mary Magdalene,
> pray for us (me).

(The names of other Saints and
Blesseds may be added.)

From all evil,
> Lord, we pray,
> deliver us (me).

From every sin,
>> Lord, we pray,
>> deliver us (me).

From the snares of the devil,
>> Lord, we pray,
>> deliver us (me).

From everlasting death,
>> Lord, we pray,
>> deliver us (me).

Christ, hear us (me).
>> Christ, hear us (me).

Christ, graciously
hear us (me).
>> Christ, graciously
>> hear us (me).

Illustrations